ATHLETICS
TRACK
by Jason Page

Barcelona '92

MAKING A SPLASH

In the steeplechase, competitors must clear 28 hurdles and 7 water jumps over a distance of 3,000 meters!

TRACK EVENTS

There are two sorts of athletic events: field events, which involve throwing or jumping, and track events, which consist entirely of races. In the Olympic Games, there are 30 different track events, and each one is covered in this book.

In short-sprint races, athletes must stay inside their own lane, but in middle- and long-distance events, they can cross over into other lanes.

Field events take place in the area inside the Olympic stadium's track.

Olympic Stadium, Atlanta, 1996

SUPER STATS

All of the track events at the 2000 Olympic Games will start and finish inside Sydney's specially built Olympic Stadium. It's the largest stadium in Olympic history, with room for 110,000 seated spectators. Four jumbo jets could fit side by side between the main arches of the grandstand!

ANCIENT ORIGINS

The first records of the ancient Olympic Games date from 776 B.C. At this time, just one competition was included. This was a track event known as the "stadion," which consisted of a 192-meter running race. The first recorded winner (and the first recorded Olympic champion) was a cook named Koroibos.

The track consists of 8 lanes. One full lap is 400 meters.

BRAVO PAAVO!

One of the greatest Olympic track athletes of all time was Paavo Nurmi (FIN), who won a total of 12 medals (nine gold and three silver) at the Games between 1920 and 1928. Nurmi competed in seven different middle- and long-distance events. Perhaps his most remarkable achievement was winning the 5,000 meters just 30 minutes after winning the 1,500 meters!

OLYMPICS FACT FILE

The Olympic Games were first held in Olympia, Greece, about 3,000 years ago. They took place every four years until they were abolished in A.D. 393.

A Frenchman named Pierre de Coubertin (1863–1937) revived the Games, and the first modern Olympics were held in Athens in 1896.

The modern Games have been held every four years since 1896, except in 1916, 1940 and 1944, due to war. Special 10th-anniversary Games took place in 1906.

The symbol of the Olympic Games is five interlocking colored rings. Together, they represent the five different continents from which athletes come to compete.

HOT STUFF

Wherever the Olympic Games go, the Olympic flame goes too! A burning torch has carried the flame to Sydney all the way from Olympia in Greece, the site of the ancient Olympic Games. Since then, teams of relay runners have carried the torch all over Australia.

Olympic flame, Seoul, 1988

RUN FOR IT

One race with ancient origins is the marathon. This was inspired by the story of an ancient Greek messenger named Pheidippides, who ran 39 kilometers to bring news of the great Battle of Marathon. Unfortunately, after delivering his message, Pheidippides died of exhaustion!

Marion Jones

GIMME FIVE

No track or field athlete has ever won five gold medals at one Olympic Games but that's exactly what sports superstar Marion Jones (USA) will be attempting to do in the Sydney Olympics. As well as setting her sights on victory in the 100 meters, Jones is also going for gold in the 200 meters, the 100-meter relay, the 400-meter relay, and the long jump!

DID YOU KNOW?

Runners in the 100 meters hold their breath until the end of the race!

In 1992, at the age of 32, Linford Christie (GBR) became the oldest person ever to win the 100 meters.

The 1900 and 1904 Olympic Games included an even shorter sprint of just 60 meters.

Starting block

The starting blocks are fitted with pressure-sensitive pads. These can detect if an athlete starts moving before the starting pistol has fired. Each athlete is allowed to make one false start — but a second offense means instant disqualification!

STARTING ORDERS

At the start of a sprint race, the official in charge shouts "On your marks." When the eight runners hear this, they kneel down and place their feet in the starting blocks. The starter then shouts "Set," at which the runners lift their hips, raise both their knees off the ground, and wait for the starter's pistol to fire.

THE 100 METERS

The shortest of the great sprint races, the 100 meters has been part of the modern Games ever since they began.

FANCY A DIP?

Have a good look at the 100 meters sprinters in action. If you watch closely, you will notice how they thrust their chests out just before they cross the finish line. This is known as "dipping." It pushes their bodies forward and knocks a couple of hundredths of a second off their time — which can mean the difference between winning gold and coming second!

SCANDAL!

A few Olympic athletes don't play by the rules. One of the worst cases of cheating occurred in the men's 100-meter final at the 1988 Olympics. Ben Johnson (CAN) was first to cross the finish line in world-record time. But just three days later, he was stripped of both his medal and the record when it was discovered that he had taken banned drugs to improve his performance.

ANIMAL OLYMPIANS

The fastest human athletes reach a top speed of around 25 mph (40 km/h), but the cheetah can knock spots off that. This powerful big cat can sprint at speeds up to 62 mph (100 km/h)!

THE 200 METERS

The first half of this race is run on a bend in the track. It requires a special sprinting skill to maintain a steady running rhythm while turning to the left!

HAVING A GOOD TIME

The reigning men's Olympic champion in the 200 meters is Michael Johnson (USA). His winning time of 19.32 seconds at the 1996 Games in Atlanta not only won him the gold medal but also set a world record!

Michael Johnson

SUPER STATS

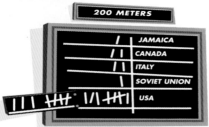

200 METERS	
/	JAMAICA
//	CANADA
//	ITALY
/	SOVIET UNION
/// ||| •/// |||	USA

The finals of the men's 200 meters have been held 22 times at the Olympics. The Soviet Union and Jamaica have both won once. Canada and Italy have each had two victories. The other 16 gold medals were won by the United States.

STAGGERING AROUND

Both the 200 meters and 400 meters have "staggered" starts. This means that instead of lining up together in a straight line (as they do in the 100 meters), the runners in the inside lanes start behind those in the outside lanes. This compensates for the curve in the track and ensures that each athlete runs exactly the same distance.

MEN'S RECORDS: WORLD: Michael Johnson (USA) 19.32 sec. **OLYMPIC:** Michael Johnson (USA) 19.32 sec.

GOLDEN RECORD

Women competed in the 200 meters for the first time in 1948. The race was won by Fanny Blankers-Koen (NED) who also won the 100 meters, the 80-meter hurdles and the 4 x 100-meter relay. Her total of four gold medals at one Games is a record for any female athlete!

Starting pistol

GOOD SHOT

The pistol used to start the 200-meter races is fired next to a microphone. The microphone carries the sound to speakers placed behind each of the starting blocks. This ensures that all the athletes hear the bang at exactly the same time. Without these speakers, the runner closest to the gun would hear it a fraction of a second before the others and get a head start.

DID YOU KNOW?

No man has ever won the 200 meters twice!

In 1904, the men's 200 meters was won by Archie Hahn (USA) after all the other runners had been given a 2-meter handicap for false starts!

In the 1932 final, one of the lanes used was 1.5 meters longer than all the others!

WOMEN'S RECORDS: WORLD: Florence Griffith-Joyner (USA) 21.34 sec. **OLYMPIC**: Florence Griffith-Joyner (USA) 21.34 sec.

Eric Liddell

GOD SPEED

Eric Liddell (GBR) won the 400 meters in 1924 despite the fact that he had spent months training for the 100 meters instead! Liddell was a devout Christian and refused to run in the 100 meters because the final was on a Sunday. Liddell believed the Bible said Sunday was to be a day of rest. Liddell not only won the 400 meters, he also broke the world record.

DID YOU KNOW?

- All races longer than 110 meters must be run counterclockwise!

- In 1984, Valerie Brisco-Hooks (USA) became the first person to win both the 200 meters and the 400 meters at the same Olympic Games!

- A film called Chariots of Fire was based on Eric Liddell's story.

THIRD TIME LUCKY?

Marie José Pérec (FRA) won the women's 400 meters at the last two Olympics, and she will be trying for a third victory in the Sydney 2000 Games. But this reigning Olympic champion will have to outrun some serious competition, including Cathy Freeman (AUS), the reigning world champion.

MEN'S RECORDS : WORLD: Michael Johnson (USA) 43.18 sec. **OLYMPIC:** Michael Johnson (USA) 43.49 sec.

THE 400 METERS

This is the longest of the sprint races and the toughest! Competitors run flat out all the way around the Olympic track.

NO COMPETITION

In 1908, the men's 400 meters was won by Wyndham Halswelle (GBR). It was the easiest victory in Olympic history, because Halswelle was the only person in the race! He ran solo in a re-run after the original winner was disqualified, and the other two finalists withdrew in protest.

LIGHT WORK

Originally, a thin piece of thread or tape was stretched across the finishing line. This has been replaced by an invisible beam of light. A sensor detects the moment that the light is broken by one of the runners crossing the line and automatically records the winning time.

Marie José Pérec

ANIMAL OLYMPIANS

Modern Olympic athletes fly around the 400-meter running track in less than 50 seconds. But a duck could fly around much faster! Ducks are among the fastest flying birds, with a top speed of over 62 mph (100 km/h). This means they would take just 14 seconds to fly 400 meters!

WOMEN'S RECORDS: WORLD: Marita Koch (GDR) 47.60 sec. **OLYMPIC:** Marie José Pérec (FRA) 48.25 sec.

THE 4 x 100-METER RELAY

This race is all about teamwork. The teams are made up of four runners who each run 100 meters—that's a quarter of the race.

TAKE THE TUBE

Instead of messages, modern relay runners carry a short hollow tube called a "baton." It's about a foot (30 cm) long and weighs at least 2 ounces (50 g)—that's about as heavy as a golf ball. If a runner drops the baton during a race, he or she must pick it up again before continuing.

SUPER STATS

The women's world record in the 4 x 100 meters is just 0.59 seconds slower than four times the women's world record for the 100 meters!

Practicing changeover

The moment when one runner passes the baton to another is called a "changeover." Relay runners spend many hours practicing their changeovers to make them as smooth and fast as possible.

MEN'S RECORDS: WORLD: United States 37.40 sec. **OLYMPIC**: United States 37.40 sec.

GET THE MESSAGE?

The origin of the relay races dates back to ancient times, when important messages were sent over long distances using teams of runners. Each messenger would run as fast as he could until he reached the next member of the team. Then he would hand over the message to his team-mate, who would run the next leg of the journey.

DID YOU KNOW?

The German team in the women's 4 x 100-meter relay missed out on a gold medal in 1936 because a runner dropped the baton!

Barbara Pearl Jones (USA) was a member of the winning U. S. team in the 1952 women's 4 x 100-meter relay. At just 15, she was the youngest track athlete ever to win a gold medal!

Jesse Owens's amazing winning streak was repeated in the same events by another American, Carl Lewis, in 1984!

Jesse Owens

GOLDEN GREAT

Jesse Owens (USA) was a member of the U. S. relay team that won the 4 x 100 meters in 1936. Owens also won gold medals in three individual events —the 100 meters, the 200 meters, and the long jump!

WOMEN'S RECORDS: WORLD: East Germany 41.37 sec. **OLYMPIC**: East Germany 41.37 sec.

SUPER STARS AND STRIPES

The men's 4 x 400-meter relay was held for the first time at the Olympics in 1912. It was won by the U. S., which has dominated the event ever since. In fact, the U. S. team has won 14 of the 19 finals. This picture shows team members celebrating their most recent victory at Atlanta in 1996.

U. S. men's 4 x 400-meter relay team

DID YOU KNOW?

¿¿ In 1988, Olga Brzygina (URS) won gold medals in the women's 4 x 400-meter relay and the 400 meters. Her husband, Viktor, won a gold in the men's 4 x 100-meter relay!

¿¿ The 4 x 400-meter relay is not run in lanes, so runners have to look behind them as they take the baton. Runners in the less chaotic 4 x 100-meters don't need to do this!

¿¿ The part of the race run by each member of a relay team is called a "leg." You could say all relay runners have one leg!

BREAKING LANES

Unlike runners in the 4 x 100-meter relay, those in the 4 x 400-meter don't have to stay in their lanes. However, they must make sure that they don't get in each others' way, particularly in the changeover zone!

Relay changeover

THE 4 x 400-METER RELAY

This relay is four times longer than the other Olympic relay race—which makes it four times as tough!

FIRST AND LAST

The first relay race ever held at the modern Olympics was a medley relay that took place in 1908. Instead of all the athletes running the same distance, the first and second runners ran 200 meters, the third ran 400 meters and the last ran 800 meters (a total of 1,600 meters). The race was won by the United States but was never held again.

ZONE LIMITS

Athletes must pass the baton to their teammate inside the changeover zone. This stretch of track is 20 meters long, and special markings show where it begins and ends. Competitors are allowed to start running before they have been handed the baton, but they mustn't pass beyond the end of the zone without it—if they do, their team will be disqualified!

SUPER STATS

Races have gotten faster and faster! The men's world record is more than 20 seconds faster than the winning time in the first Olympic 4 x 400-meter relay, held in 1912.

THE 800 METERS

This is the first of the two middle-distance races held at the Olympics. It is a test of stamina as well as speed.

GIRL POWER

The men's 800 meters has been held at every single Olympic Games. The women's event was introduced in 1928, but it wasn't held again until 1960 because the men who organized the Olympics were worried that women weren't strong enough to run such a long race. Female athletes have since proved them wrong — in fact, the women's 800-meter record is 18 seconds faster than the winning time in the men's event of 1896!

RUNNING FLAT OUT

The longer the race, the more exhausting it is for the runner. In the 1996 Games, Vebjorn Rodal (NOR) had used up all his strength by the end of the men's 800-meter final, as the picture at right shows. He won the gold medal and set an Olympic record!

Vebjorn Rodal

ANIMAL OLYMPIANS

The common flea can cover 220 times the length of its own body with one leap. If humans could do the same, we would be able to complete the 800 meters with just two leaps!

BOXING MATCH

Tactics play a big part in winning a race. A runner who doesn't watch out can end up being boxed in — in other words, surrounded by a group of other runners and prevented from taking the lead. This is what has happened to the runner wearing number 151 in the picture.

ON THE BALL

At the 1992 Games, the gold medal in the women's 800 meters was won by Ellen Van Langen (NED). However, Langen began her sporting career not as a runner but as a soccer player! Four years before her Olympic triumph, she was playing for Holland's national women's team.

DID YOU KNOW?

The 800 meters begins with a staggered start. Once the runners pass the first bend, they are allowed to disregard their lanes and move to the inside of the track.

In 1992, the gold and silver medalists in the 800-meter men's final were separated by only 4/100th of a second!

The 1928 women's 800 meters was won by 24-year-old Lina Radke-Batschauer (GER). It was the first individual gold medal won by a German competitor at the Olympics!

WOMEN'S RECORDS: WORLD: Jarmila Kratochvílová (TCH) 1 min. 53.28 sec. **OLYMPIC:** Nadezhda Olizarenko (URS) 1 min. 53.43 sec.

THE 1,500 METERS

The men's 1,500-meter race has been part of every Olympics since the modern Games began, but the women's event was not introduced until 1972.

DOING THE DOUBLE

So far, seven athletes have won both middle-distance races at the same Games. Svetlana Masterkova (RUS), pictured right, is the most recent. She took the gold in the 800 meters and the 1,500 meters at Atlanta in 1996.

Svetlana Masterkova

All athletes must wear a number on their clothing. This is used by race officials to identify them.

A runner's clothing needs to be light and flexible. Tight-fitting clothes make the athlete's body more streamlined and aerodynamic.

Start of the 1,500 meters

GETTING GOING

Unlike shorter races, the 1,500 meters doesn't begin with a staggered start. Instead, runners form a curved line across the track and are allowed to break from their lanes as soon as the starting pistol is fired.

Runners wear lightweight shoes with short spikes on the sole. The spikes, which must not be longer than half an inch (12 mm), grip the track and stop the athlete from slipping.

SUPER STATS

The diplodocus was one of the longest dinosaurs that ever roamed the Earth, but it wasn't nearly as long as the 1,500-meter race! In fact, you would need more than 55 of these giant dinos placed nose-to-tail to reach from the start to the finish line.

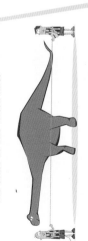

SHORT-SPRINT HURDLES

The short-sprint hurdles race requires total concentration. The smallest mistake can lead to disaster—as athlete Gail Devers discovered!

SPOT THE DIFFERENCE

In all hurdle races, there are 10 hurdles to jump. The difference is in the height of the hurdle and the length of the track. The men's short-sprint event is 110 meters long—10 meters longer than the women's event. The men's hurdles are also slightly higher—42 inches (106.7 cm) compared to 33 inches (83.8 cm).

GOING...

GOING...

GONE...

Gail Devers

FALLING AT THE FINAL HURDLE

In the 1992 Games, Gail Devers (USA) was in the lead during the final of the 100-meter hurdles when she hit the last hurdle with her foot. This mistake cost her the race. She lost her balance, stumbled, and fell over the line in fifth place. Five days earlier, Devers had won the 100-meter sprint. Had she also won the hurdles, she would have become the first woman in Olympic history to take the gold in both events.

Allen Johnson, the reigning men's short-sprint hurdles Olympic champion, holds his daughter after winning the gold and setting an Olympic record at the 1996 Atlanta Games.

UP, UP, & AWAY!

As a hurdler leaps over a jump, he or she pushes the front leg straight out ahead.

The other leg follows knee-first and is kept bent, sweeping low and flat over the top of the hurdle. Hurdlers must spend hours practicing their jumping technique to ensure a perfectly smooth running rhythm.

DID YOU KNOW?

In both the men's and the women's short-sprint hurdles, athletes take three strides between each jump.

Hurdlers are allowed to knock the hurdles down, but if their foot passes by the side of a hurdle below the height of the crossbar, they are disqualified.

Until 1968, the women's short-sprint hurdles race was just 80 meters long.

THE ONE & ONLY

Only one athlete has ever won both the 400 meters and 400-meter hurdles. Harry Hillman (USA) achieved this remarkable feat back in 1904. However, the hurdles used in Hillman's race were 6 inches (15 cm) shorter than the hurdles used in Sydney.

MIGHTY MOSES

Edwin Moses (USA) won the men's 400-meter hurdles at the 1976 Olympics and set a world record. The following year, he began a winning streak that lasted almost 10 years! He won every single one of his next 122 races, including another Olympic gold in 1984.

Edwin Moses

DID YOU KNOW?

The hurdles in the 400 meters are lower than the ones used in the short-sprint hurdles—35.6 inches (91.4 cm) high in the men's event and 29.7 inches (76.2 cm) high in the women's.

Hurdles are designed so that they will fall over when the crossbar is hit by a force of at least 7.9 pounds (3.6 kg).

Edwin Moses might have won another gold in 1980, but the U. S. did not compete in the Games that year because of a political protest.

WARM-UP TECHNIQUES

All athletes have to warm up before they compete to help prevent injuries such as torn muscles. A good warm-up exercise for hurdlers is called "ground hurdling." This involves sitting down with one leg stretched out in front and the other bent around behind, then bending forward as far as possible. Stretching a leg out along the top of a hurdle is also a good way to warm up!

THE 400-METER HURDLES

The hurdles are shorter in this race, but sprinting for 400 meters is a big part of the challenge!

In the 400-meter event, the hurdles are placed 40 meters apart. Edwin Moses was capable of covering this distance in just 13 strides!

Tony Jarrett
(GBR)

At 29.7 inches (76.2 cm) high, the hurdles used in the women's 400-meters are about half as tall as you are. But even the shortest hurdles are a tall order if you have to jump over 10 of them in a row!

SUPER STATS

WOMEN'S RECORDS: WORLD: Kim Batten (USA) 52.61 sec. **OLYMPIC**: Deon Hemmings (JAM) 52.82 sec.

THE STEEPLECHASE

At 3,000 meters long and with 28 hurdles and 7 water jumps to clear, the steeplechase is positively a hurdling marathon!

LEADING THE CHARGE

This picture shows Joseph Keter (KEN) lagging behind his countryman Moses Kiptanui in the 1996 Atlanta Games, but Keter then went on to win the race! Kenya has dominated this event in recent years, winning golds at four Olympic games in a row. In fact, at the 1992 Games in Barcelona, all three medals were won by Kenyan athletes.

ANIMAL OLYMPIANS

The steeplechase is named after a type of horse race that involves jumping over hedges and ditches. If horses were to race against humans, they would gallop away with the gold. They can run twice as fast and can clear jumps two-and-a-half times higher than the steeplechase hurdles.

Unlike the other hurdles, these are sturdy and can't topple over.

MEN'S 110-METERS
height:
3 ft, 6 in
106.7 cm

WOMEN'S 100-METERS
height:
2 ft, 9 in
83.8 cm

MAKING A SPLASH

Competitors jump straight over the hurdles, but when they come to the water jump, they step on the crossbar. Leaping from the top of the barrier enables them to jump farther and clear more of the water. However, it's impossible not to land with a splash, and everyone ends up with wet feet!

LANDING IN DEEP WATER

The bottom of the water trough is sloped so that the water gets shallower the farther you jump. The trough is deepest near the hurdle. The water here is 27 inches (70 cm) deep. If you stood in it, it would come up to your middle!

Joseph Keter

DID YOU KNOW?

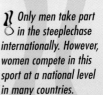

Only men take part in the steeplechase internationally. However, women compete in this sport at a national level in many countries.

To cover 3,000 meters takes 7.5 laps of the running track. Each lap has four hurdles and one water jump.

In the 1932 Olympics, the winner of the steeplechase ran an extra lap by mistake!

HURDLING HEIGHTS

Steeplechase hurdles are the same height as those used in the men's 400-meter hurdles race. The hurdles are 13 feet (3.96 meters) wide — much wider than the hurdles used in other races. This is because all the competitors go over the same jumps.

STEEPLECHASE
ght: 3 feet (91.4 cm)
th: 13 feet (3.96 m)

MEN'S 400-METERS
height:
3 ft
91.4 cm

WOMEN'S 400-METERS
height:
2 ft, 6 in
76.2 cm

LONG WAIT

Women athletes had to wait until 1984 before they could take part in long-distance races at the Olympics. A 3,000-meter race and women's marathon were finally introduced when the Games were in Los Angeles in 1984. Four years later, in Seoul, women were allowed to compete in the 10,000 meters for the first time. In the Atlanta Olympics, the women's 3,000 meters was replaced by the 5,000 meters — which means, at long last, the women's and men's long-distance events are the same!

Wang Jun Xia

DID YOU KNOW?

Athletes are given their medals in a grand ceremony in front of the crowd, but when the modern Olympics first started, medals were sometimes mailed to the winners!

Athletes in middle- and long-distance races are not allowed to use starting blocks.

There used to be a 5,000-meter team race. It was held only once, in 1900, when it was won by a team made up of British and Australian runners.

MEN'S RECORDS: WORLD: Haile Gebrselassie (ETH) 12 min. 39.36 sec. **OLYMPIC**: Said Aouita (MAR) 13 min. 05.59 sec.

THE 5,000 METERS

When the going gets tough, the tough get going. And in a 5,000-meter race, they've got a long way to go!

WANG WINS

The reigning women's 5,000 meters Olympic champion is Wang Jun Xia (CHN). Her winning time at Atlanta (1996) was just a fraction of a second under 15 minutes and set an Olympic record.

IN TRAINING

Long-distance races test the athletes' fitness and stamina to the limits. Competitors have to spend countless hours training, and they run up to 93 miles (150 km) every week in order to stay in peak condition. That's the same as 375 laps of an Olympic running track!

FAMOUS FIVE

Five athletes have won both the 5,000 meters and the 10,000 meters at the same Games. Vladimir Kuts (URS) achieved this remarkable double when the Olympics were last held in Australia, in 1956.

ANIMAL OLYMPIANS

The pronghorn antelope is the long-distance running champion of the animal kingdom. It can maintain a steady speed of 35 mph (56 km/h) for a distance of 3 miles (5 km). No other animal can travel so far, so fast!

Vladimir Kuts

WOMEN'S RECORDS: WORLD: Jiang Bo (CHN) 14 min. 28.09 sec. **OLYMPIC:** Wang Jun Xia (CHN) 14 min 59.88 sec.

THE 10,000 METERS

This is the longest race held inside the Olympic stadium. Athletes have to run 25 laps around the track!

AFRICA UNITED

In 1992, athletes from South Africa were able to compete at the Olympic Games for the first time in 32 years! They had been banned because of their government's apartheid policy, which kept black and white people apart. However, when this policy was ended, so was the ban. Elana Meyer (RSA) celebrated her country's return to the Games with a silver medal in the women's 10,000 meters, finishing six seconds behind Derartu Tulu (ETH).

SUPER STATS

Traveling at top speed without taking any rests, it would take a garden snail more than eight days to finish the 10,000 meters!

Elana Meyer

THINKING WITH YOUR FEET

Winning a long-distance race requires mental tactics as well as physical stamina. Runners have to plan how they are going to use their energy reserves. Some try to surprise their opponents with a sudden burst of speed a whole lap before the end of the race, while others save their energy for the final sprint just before the finish.

DID YOU KNOW?

? The world record in the 10,000 meters is 5 minutes faster than the winning time in the 1912 Olympics!

? Finland has won the men's 10,000 meters more times than any other country, with seven victories to its credit.

? The 10,000-meter race takes more than 160 times longer to run than the 100-meter race!

SETTING THE PACE

World records in long-distance events are rarely broken at the Olympic Games. This is because all of the competitors are trying to win, so there's usually no one to act as a "pacemaker" — someone who leads the race at the beginning and sets a fast pace for the others to follow. Pacemakers help other athletes break records but because they start out so quickly, they are usually exhausted before they reach the finish line.

HALE HAILE!

Haile Gebreselassie (ETH), the reigning 10,000-meter men's Olympic champion and world record holder, will be ready to defend his title at Sydney. He also holds the world record in the 5,000 meters.

Haile Gebreselassie

WOMEN'S RECORDS: WORLD: Wang Jun Xia (CHN) 29 min. 31.78 sec. OLYMPIC: Fernanda Ribeiro (POR) 31 min. 1.63 sec.

FANCY A LONG WALK?

Walking races are very long! The women's event is usually 10 kilometers, but at the Games in Sydney, the distance has been doubled. There are two men's events. One is the 20 kilometers and the other is the whopping 50 kilometers. That's longer than the marathon!

Women's 10-km walk

DID YOU KNOW?

The 50-km walk is the equivalent of 125 laps of the Olympic track.

There have been several other walking events in Olympic history—including a 1,500-meter walk!

Walking races start and finish in the Olympic stadium but most of the race takes place on the surrounding streets.

WIGGLE IT!

By swinging their hips from side to side, walkers can increase the length of their stride. This means they travel farther with each step, but it also means they look quite silly!

Andrzej Chylinski (USA)

MEN'S RECORDS: WORLD: 20-km: Bernardo Segura (MEX) 1 hr. 17 min. 25.6 sec. / 50-km: Andrey Perlov (RUS) 3 hr. 37 mi. 41 sec.
OLYMPIC: 20-km: Jozef Pribilinec (TCH) 1 hr. 19 min. 57 sec. / 50-km: Vyacheslav Ivanenko (URS) 3 hr. 38 min. 29 sec.

WALKING RACES

Walking races sound easy enough but there's a lot more to them than you might think!

LEARNING TO WALK

In a walking race, the rule is that you must keep one foot on the ground at all times. In other words, you must not lift your back foot up until you've put your front foot down. Your back leg must also be straightened for a moment while your back foot is on the ground. Try it — it's not as easy as it sounds, especially if you're trying to walk quickly.

WARNING SIGNALS

Judges keep a close eye on the walkers. If a competitor is spotted breaking the rules, the judge will show a disk as a warning. If the competitor then commits a second offense, another disk will be raised to signal that he or she has been disqualified.

Medal-winning walkers achieve an average speed of more than 9 mph (15 km/h). That's half as fast as a sprint champion but twice as fast as an Olympic swimmer!

SUPER STATS

THE MARATHON

The marathon is a grueling run through the streets of the Olympic city. This event is the ultimate test of stamina and determination!

BY ROYAL COMMAND

The first modern Olympic marathons were 25 miles (40 km) long. However, when the Games came to London in 1908, the race was lengthened slightly to 26.2 miles (42.195 km) because the British royal family wanted to watch the start of the race in front of Windsor Castle! This distance was then adopted as the official length of the Olympic marathon.

ANIMAL OLYMPIANS

When it comes to marathon journeys, the annual trip across North America by the caribou takes some beating. These large deer travel up to 25,000 miles (40,000 km) every year—the equivalent of almost 1,000 marathon races.

25,000 m

Lee Bong Ju

Dorando Pietri

NOT FAIR!

Dorando Pietri (ITA) was the unluckiest marathon runner in Olympic history. At the Games in 1908, Pietri was leading the race as he entered the Olympic stadium. However, he collapsed from exhaustion four times on the final lap of the track. Eventually, two race officials helped him across the finish line. Although Pietri finished first, he was disqualified because the judges said he had "used external support," which is against the rules!

SOUTH AFRICA
Atlanta 1996
2122

Josia Thugwane

TIRED YET?

The reigning Olympic champion Josia Thugwane (RSA) still had enough energy after winning the marathon to take a victory lap around the track with Lee Bong Ju (KOR), who took the silver medal.

THIRSTY WORK

Officials give water to the runners 7 miles (11 km) into the race and then every 3 miles (5 km) or so after that. Wet sponges are also handed out at regular intervals to help keep the runners cool.

DID YOU KNOW?

The first modern Olympic marathon was won by a penniless Greek shepherd in 1896. As well as a gold medal, he was presented with a horse and cart for his village!

Marathon world and Olympic records are regarded as "unofficial" because each marathon course is slightly different.

In the 1988 marathon, 118 runners took part—the largest number of people ever to compete in a single Olympic event!

WOMEN'S RECORDS: WORLD: Tegla Loroupe (KEN) 2 hr. 20 min. 43 sec. OLYMPIC: Joan Benoit (USA) 2 hr. 24 min. 52 sec.

INDEX

Acknowledgments

We would like to thank Ian Hodge, Richard Mead and Elizabeth Wiggans for their assistance. Cartoons by John Alston.
Copyright © 2000 *ticktock* Publishing Ltd. Printed in Hong Kong.
First published in Great Britain by ticktock Publishing Ltd., The Offices in the Square, Hadlow, Tonbridge, Kent TN11 0DD, Great Britain.
Picture Credits: All images courtesy of (c) Allsport. Picture research by Image Select.

Library of Congress Cataloging-in-Publishing Data

Page, Jason.
    Athletics, Track : 100 meters, 200 meters, relays, hurdles, and lots, lots more / by Jason Page.
        p. cm. -- (Zeke's Olympic pocket guide)
Includes index.
Summary: Describes the track events of the Olympic Games and previews the athletic competition at the 2000 Summer Olympics in Sydney,
Australia.
    ISBN 0-8225-5054-7 (pbk. : alk. paper)
1. Track-athletics--Juvenile literature. 2. Running--Juvenile literature. 3. Olympics--Juvenile literature. [1. Track and field. 2. Running. 3.
Olympics.] I. Title. II. Series.
    GV1060.5 .P26 2000
    796.42--dc21
                                                                            00-008457